Saint Brigid of Kildare: The Legacy of One of Ireland's Patron Saints

By Charles River Editors

St. Bride by John Duncan

About Charles River Editors

Charles River Editors is a boutique digital publishing company, specializing in bringing history back to life with educational and engaging books on a wide range of topics. Keep up to date with our new and free offerings with [this 5 second sign up on our weekly mailing list](), and visit [Our Kindle Author Page]() to see other recently published Kindle titles.

We make these books for you and always want to know our readers' opinions, so we encourage you to leave reviews and look forward to publishing new and exciting titles each week.

Introduction

A depiction of Saint Brigid in Saint Non's Chapel, St Davids (Wales)

"It is a virtue and a prize to listen patiently to and put up with insults for the sake of God." – Saint Brigid of Kildare

The drumbeat of horses' hooves and clatter of chariot wheels echo through the rolling green hills of what will be known much later as the Emerald Isle. The driver is a lone woman whose long hair and homespun cloak whip through the wind behind her. Headstrong, confident, and intelligent, she blazes a trail that will change her nation forevermore, yet not in her own name or for her own sake, but for that of the God who sent her. This is a woman who will love the poor, feed the hungry, house the homeless, teach the ignorant, and defy the odds doing it all. This is Brigid of Kildare.

Saint Brigid of Kildare survives as a model of the religious life, a woman who cared for the earth and its people, who strove for justice, equality, and peace. She is also a model of the disciple's life, one who took Christ's Great Commission to heart, traversing her nation to welcome other men and women into the fold and encourage the spread of Christianity wherever she went, through the gospel message of love for one's neighbor and God's saving grace. Because her legends trace back to pre-Christian times, Brigid is one of the most powerful religious figures in all of Irish history, as her story intertwines many layers of separate traditions, both pagan and Christian.

That said, even as her story remains mixed with folk tales and pagan customs, along with St. Patrick, Brigid is credited with the evangelization of the entire Irish nation, turning the pagan island into a bastion of Catholic Christianity. She is often seen as a bridge between pagan and Christian Irish traditions, bringing commonality to a world divided by religious beliefs. She also represents a bridge between social classes, as she was the daughter of a king and a leading religious authority, but administered to the poorest of people and the lowliest of creatures. She welcomed kings and paupers, saints and pagans, and men and women into her fold, seeing the light of Christ in all of God's creations.

Saint Brigid of Kildare: The Life, Legends, and Legacy of One of Ireland's Patron Saints chronicles Brigid's story, and how she became one of the most famous saints in history. Along with pictures depicting important people, places, and events, you will learn about Brigid of Kildare like never before.

Saint Brigid of Kildare: The Life, Legends, and Legacy of One of Ireland's Patron Saints

About Charles River Editors

Introduction

  The Celtic Goddess

  The Life of Brigid

  Conversion

  The Church that Brigid Built

  Brigidine Sisters

  St. Brigid's Legacy

  Online Resources

  Bibliography

Free Books by Charles River Editors

Discounted Books by Charles River Editors

The Celtic Goddess

It's impossible to truly understand the impact of Saint Brigid without knowing about her pagan predecessor, Brid. When the Celtic people from central Europe invaded the British Isles in the 7th century BCE, they brought their Druidic religion with them.

People love reading about the Druids, yet many would have a hard time even defining them, and there is even considerable debate about the etymology of the word "Druid." Thankfully, there are plenty of ancient sources of information documenting the existence of the Druids, and there is also archaeological evidence. It is from the written record, specifically the writings of Roman chroniclers, that people first learned about the Druids, and ultimately it is from these important but questionable sources that scholars have the only confirmed evidence about the beliefs and practices of the ancient Druids.

Even before the rise of the Roman Empire, ancient historians described the Celts and some of their rituals. According to the ancient Greek historian Athenaeus, in the 4th century BCE, Sopater noted, "Among them is the custom, whenever they are victorious in battle, to sacrifice their prisoners to the gods. So I, like the Celts, have vowed to the divine powers to burn those three false dialecticians as an offering." In the early 3rd century BCE,

Timaeus wrote, "Historians point out that the Celts who live on the shore of the Ocean honor the Dioscori above other gods. For there is an ancient tradition among them that these gods came to them from the Ocean."

Another Greek historian noted their use of sacrifices: "Eudoxus says that the Celts do the following (and if anyone thinks his account credible, let him believe it; if not, let him ignore it). When clouds of locusts invade their country and damage the crops, the Celts evoke certain prayers and offer sacrifices which charm birds—and the birds hear these prayers, come in flocks, and destroy the locusts. If however one of them should capture one of these birds, his punishment according to the laws of the country is death. If he is pardoned and released, this throws the birds into a rage, and to revenge the captured bird they do not respond if they are called on again." Strabo noted a similar anecdote: "The following story which Artemidorus has told about the crows is unbelievable. There is a certain harbor on the coast which, according to him, is named 'Two Crows'. In this harbor are seen two crows, with their right wings somewhat white. Men who are in dispute about certain matters come here, put a plank on an elevated place, and then each man separately throws up cakes of barley. The birds fly up and eat some of the cakes, but scatter others. The man whose cakes are scattered wins the dispute. Although this story is implausible, his report about the goddesses Demeter and Core is more credible. He says that there is an island near Britain on which sacrifices are performed like those in Samothrace for Demeter and Core."

Ultimately, the most concrete descriptions of the Druids came from several Roman writers, who offer tantalizing glimpses into the lost religious and ritual world of the Druids and overwhelmingly demonstrate the social power that the Druids had and the ways that Romans seemed to often hold them in awe as well. Perhaps the most detailed discussion of the Druids and their ways comes from Julius Caesar's *Notebooks About the Gallic War*, written some time in the 50s or 40s BC. He discusses Celtic society and the Druids at length:

> "Throughout Gaul there are two classes of persons of definite account and dignity…Of the two classes above mentioned one consists of Druids, the other of knights. The former are concerned with divine worship, the due performance of sacrifices, public and private, and the interpretation of ritual questions: a great number of young men gather about them for the sake of instruction and hold them in great honour.
>
> "A great many young men come to the Druids for instruction, holding them in great respect.

Indeed, the Druids are the judges on all controversies public and private. If any crime has been committed, if any murder done, if there are any questions concerning inheritance, or any controversy concerning boundaries, the Druids decide the case and determine punishments. If anyone ignores their decision, that person is banned from all sacrifices—an extremely harsh punishment among the Gauls. Those who are so condemned are considered detestable criminals. Everyone shuns them and will not speak with them, fearing some harm from contact with them, and they receive no justice nor honor for any worthy deed.

"Among all the Druids there is one who is the supreme leader, holding highest authority over the rest. When the chief Druid dies, whoever is the most worthy succeeds him. If there are several of equal standing, a vote of all the Druids follows, though the leadership is sometimes contested even by armed force. At a certain time of the year, all the Druids gather together at a consecrated spot in the territory of the Carnutes, whose land is held to be the center of all Gaul. Everyone gathers therefrom the whole land to present disputes and they obey the judgments and decrees of the Druids. It is said that the Druidic movement began in Britain and was then carried across to Gaul. Even today, those who wish to study their teachings most diligently usually travel to Britain.

"The Druids are exempt from serving in combat and from paying war taxes, unlike all other Gauls. Tempted by such advantages, many young people willingly commit themselves to Druidic studies while others are sent by their parents. It is said that in the schools of the Druids they learn a great number of verses, so many in fact that some students spend twenty years in training. It is not permitted to write down any of these sacred teachings, though other public and private transactions are often recorded in Greek letters. I believe they practice this oral tradition for two reasons: first, so that the common crowd does not gain access to their secrets and second, to improve the faculty of memory. Truly, writing does often weaken one's diligence in learning and reduces the ability to memorize. The cardinal teaching of the Druids is that the soul does not perish, but after death passes from one body to another. Because of this teaching that death is only a transition, they are able to encourage fearlessness in battle. They have a great many other teachings as well which they hand down to the young concerning such things as the motion of the stars, the size of the cosmos and the earth, the order of the natural world, and the power of the immortal gods.

"All of the Gauls are greatly devoted to religion, and because of this those who are afflicted with terrible illnesses or face dangers in battle will conduct human sacrifices, or at least vow to do so. The Druids are the ministers at such occasions. They believe that unless the life of a person is offered for the life of another, the dignity of the immortal gods will be insulted. This is true both in private and public sacrifices. Some build enormous figures which they fill with living persons and then set on fire, everyone perishing inflames. They believe that the execution of thieves and other criminals is the most pleasing to the gods, but, when the supply of guilty persons runs short, they will kill the innocent as well.

"The chief god of the Gauls is Mercury and there are images of him everywhere. He is said to be the inventor of all the arts, the guide for every road and journey, and the most influential god in trade and moneymaking. After him, they worship Apollo, Mars, Jupiter, and Minerva. These gods have the same areas of influence as among most other peoples. Apollo drives away diseases, Minerva is most influential in crafts, Jupiter rules the sky, and Mars is the god of war. Before a great battle, they will often dedicate the spoils to Mars. If they are successful, they will sacrifice all the living things they have captured and other spoils they gather together in one place. Among many tribes, you can see these spoils placed together in a sacred spot. And it is a very rare occasion that anyone would dare to disturb these valuable goods and conceal them in his home. If it does happen, the perpetrator is tortured and punished in the worst ways imaginable.

"The Gauls all say that they are descended from the god of the dark underworld, Dis, and confirm that this is the teaching of the Druids. Because of this they measure time by the passing of nights, not days. Birthdays and the beginnings of months and years all start at night.

"The funerals of the Gauls are magnificent and extravagant. Everything which was dear to the departed is thrown into the fire, including animals. In the recent past, they would also burn faithful slaves and beloved subordinates at the climax of the funeral."[1]

Caesar, while writing something of a puff-piece in *Notebooks*, certainly had firsthand knowledge of the Druids from his time fighting the Gauls and was thus an invaluable direct observer. While probably writing from second-hand sources, Strabo gave a similar description of the Druids' high status in his seminal *Geography*, which was published in the first decade of the 1st century BCE, before Caesar's work: "Among all the Gallic peoples, generally speaking, there are three sets of men who are held in exceptional honour; the Bards, the Vates and the Druids. The Bards are singers and poets; the Vates, diviners and natural philosophers; while the Druids, in addition to natural philosophy, study also moral philosophy."[2]

Caesar's observation that the Druids acted like judges for social disputes was also echoed by Strabo, who wrote, "The Druids are considered the most just of men, and on this account they are entrusted with the decision, not only of the private disputes, but of the public disputes as well; so that, in former times, they even arbitrated cases of war and made the opponents stop when they were about to line

---

[1] All of the Caesar quotes are from: *The Gallic War* by Julius Caesar, Book VI Chapters 13-14. Accessed online at:
http://penelope.uchicago.edu/Thayer/E/Roman/Texts/Caesar/Gallic_War/6B*.html#13
[2] All of the Strabo quotes come from *The Geography Book IV, Chapter 4:4* accessed online at:
http://penelope.uchicago.edu/Thayer/E/Roman/Texts/Strabo/4D*.html#4.4

up for battle, and the murder cases, in particular, had been turned over to them for decision. Further, when there is a big yield from these cases, there is forthcoming a big yield from the land too, as they think." Strabo also seems to confirm Caesar's description of the Druids' religious beliefs about the immortality of the soul: "However, not only the Druids, but others as well, say that men's souls, and also the universe, are indestructible, although both fire and water will at some time or other prevail over them."

While these theological points may have been of some interest to the Romans, one area of religious practice that always intrigued ancient writers was divination: the ability to tell the future or of far off events. The famous Roman orator and philosopher Cicero described the Druids, amongst the religious practitioners of several foreign peoples, in his work *De Divinatione* *("Of Divination")*. He wrote, in approximately 44 BCE, "Nor is the practice of divination disregarded even among uncivilized tribes, if indeed there are Druids in Gaul — and there are, for I knew one of them myself, Divitiacus, the Aeduan, your guest and eulogist. He claimed to have that knowledge of nature which the Greeks call 'physiologia,' and he used to make predictions, sometimes by means of augury and sometimes by means of conjecture."[3] Strabo also

---

[3] *De Divinatione* Book I 41:90, accessed online at:
http://penelope.uchicago.edu/Thayer/E/Roman/Texts/Cicero/de_Divinatione/1*.html

mentioned Druidic divination: "They used to strike a human being, whom they had devoted to death, in the back with a sabre, and then divine from his death-struggle. But they would not sacrifice without the Druids."[4]

Diodorus Sicilus described Druidic rituals surrounding divination at length:

> "The Gauls have certain wise men and experts on the gods called Druids, as well as a highly respected class of seers. Through auguries and animal sacrifice these seers predict the future and no one dares to scoff at them. They have an especially odd and unbelievable method of divination for the most important matters. Having anointed a human victim, they stab him with a small knife in the area above the diaphragm. When the man has collapsed from the wound, they interpret the future by observing the nature of his fall, the convulsion of his limbs, and especially from the pattern of his spurting blood. In this type of divination, the seers place great trust in an ancient tradition of observation.
>
> "It is a custom among the Gauls to never perform a sacrifice without someone skilled in divine ways present. They say that those who

---

[4] Strabo's *The Geography Book IV, Chapter 4:5*

know about the nature of the gods should offer thanks to them and make requests of them, as though these people spoke the same language as the gods. The Gauls, friends and foes alike, obey the rule of the priests and bards not only in time of peace but also during wars. It has often happened that just as two armies approached each other with swords drawn and spears ready, the Druids will step between the two sides and stop the fighting, as if they had cast a spell on wild beasts. Thus even among the wildest barbarians, anger yields to wisdom and the god of war respects the Muses…

"It is in keeping with their wildness and savage nature that they carry out particularly offensive religious practices. They will keep some criminal under guard for five years, then impale him on a pole in honor of their gods—followed by burning him on an enormous pyre along with many other first-fruits. They also use prisoners of war as sacrifices to the gods. Some of the Gauls will even sacrifice animals captured in war, either by slaying them, burning them, or by killing them with some other type of torture."

A better-known account of their divinatory and magical practices comes from *The Natural History*, by Pliny the

Elder, who mentions the Druids in his chapter on mistletoe. He noted:

> "I can't forget to mention the admiration the Gauls have for mistletoe. The Druids (which is the name of their holy men) hold nothing more sacred than this plant and the tree on which it grows—as if it grew only on oaks. They worship only in oak groves and will perform no sacred rites unless a branch of that tree is present. It seems the Druids even get their name from drus (the Greek word for oak). And indeed they think that anything which grows on an oak tree is sent from above and is a sign that the tree was selected by the god himself. The problem is that in fact mistletoe rarely grows on oak trees. Still they search it out with great diligence and then will cut it only on the sixth day of the moon's cycle, because the moon is then growing in power but is not yet halfway through its course (they use the moon to measure not only months but years and their grand cycle of thirty years). In their language they call mistletoe a name meaning "all-healing". They hold sacrifices and sacred meals under oak trees, first leading forward two white bulls with horns bound for the first time. A priest dressed in white then climbs

the tree and cuts the mistletoe with a golden sickle, with the plant dropping onto a white cloak. They then sacrifice the bulls while praying that the god will favorably grant his own gift to those to whom he has given it. They believe a drink made with mistletoe will restore fertility to barren livestock and act as a remedy to all poisons. Such is the devotion to frivolous affairs shown by many peoples.

"Similar to the Sabine herb savin is a plant called selago. It must be picked without an iron instrument by passing the right hand through the opening of the left sleeve, as if you were stealing it. The harvester, having first offered bread and wine, must wear white and have clean, bare feet. It is carried in a new piece of cloth. The Druids of Gaul say that it is should be used to ward off every danger and that the smoke of burning selago is good for eye diseases. The Druids also gather a plant from marshes called samolus, which must be picked with the left hand during a time of fasting. It is good for the diseases of cows, but the one who gathers it must not look back nor place it anywhere except in the watering trough of the animals.

"There is a kind of egg which is very famous in

Gaul but ignored by Greek writers. In the summer months, a vast number of snakes will gather themselves together in a ball which is held together by their saliva and a secretion from their bodies. The Druids say they produce this egg-like object called an anguinum which the hissing snakes throw up into the air. It must be caught, so they say, in a cloak before it hits the ground. But you'd better have a horse handy, because the snakes will chase you until they are cut off by some stream. A genuine anguinum will float upstream, even if covered in gold. But as is common with the world's holy men, the Druids say it can only be gathered during a particular phase of the moon, as if people could make the moon and serpents work together. I saw one of these eggs myself—it was a small round thing like an apple with a hard surface full of indentations as on the arms of an octopus. The Druids value them highly. They say it is a great help in lawsuits and will help you gain the good will of a ruler. That this is plainly false is shown by a man of the Gaulish Vocontii tribe, a Roman knight, who kept one hidden in his cloak during a trial before the emperor Claudius and was executed, as far as I can tell, for this reason alone.

"Barbarous rites were found in Gaul even within my own memory. For it was then that the emperor Tiberius passed a decree through the senate outlawing their Druids and these types of diviners and physicians. But why do I mention this about a practice which has crossed the sea and reached the ends of the earth? For even today Britain performs rites with such ceremony that you would think they were the source for the extravagant Persians. It is amazing how distant people are so similar in such practices. But at least we can be glad that the Romans have wiped out the murderous cult of the Druids, who thought human sacrifice and ritual cannibalism were the greatest kind of piety."[5]

In this excerpt, Pliny offers perhaps the richest detail of all of the ancient sources. His account includes details of Druidic ritual - the use of oak groves, the importance of mistletoe - that were not noted anywhere else, and it's perhaps no coincidence that worship in oaken groves was not unique to the Druids, as there is evidence that the Germanic god Thor/Donar was worshiped primarily in this context as well.[6]

Perhaps most importantly, Pliny provides an evocative

---

[5] *Natural History* by Pliny the Elder, Volume 3, Book XVI: Chapter 95
[6] *Thor: The Origins, History and Evolution of the Norse God* by Jesse Harasta (2013). Charles River Editors.

image that has influenced all later images of the Druids: a white-robed priest with a golden sickle climbing an oak tree to harvest mistletoe while two white bulls bellow on the floor of the grove below.[7] He also notes that the Druids used a lunar calendar that began their months on the fifth day of the lunar cycle and was divided up into months, years and 'ages[8].' The Romans, on the other hand, used a solar calendar that they dated back to the founding of their city ("the Calendar of Romulus"), and a revised form of that calendar is still used across the West today. The existence of a calendar is itself a tribute to the Druids' learning and their ability to not only carefully track celestial motions but also perform relatively complex mathematics; the fact that they apparently did so without writing is even more impressive (though not unique, as the civilizations of the Andes also created elaborate calendars without writing).[9]

In total, these written accounts all create a rough outline of the Druids that seems to describe a pan-Celtic order of priests and political functionaries who performed rituals in oak groves using mistletoe. These accounts also suggest the Druids were central to sacred sacrifices, were keepers

---

[7] A sickle is a hand tool with a handle and a curved blade perhaps as long as a forearm. It was used for harvesting grain and hay.
[8] An 'age' here is a roughly defined term, but it may refer to a larger cycle of events akin to the cyclical events in the Mesoamerican Long Count calendar. As the Druids apparently taught about the eternal, yet constantly renewing, nature of the earth, it is possible that Ages were seen as 'restarts' in the celestial cycles.
[9] "Mesoamerican Writing Systems" at Ancientscripts.com, accessed online at: http://www.ancientscripts.com/ma_ws.html

of a vast body of knowledge (including a calendar) through memorization, especially the theological concept of metempsychosis (the undeath of the soul and reincarnation). Druids also apparently served as neutral arbitrators and diplomats for the fractious Celtic chiefdoms. The ancient accounts are supported by the weak linguistic evidence that interprets the word "Druid" as originating from term meaning "those who know the oak" and "truth" in Old Celtic.

One of the most important observations that emerges from the Roman accounts is that the Druids had two distinct roles within society, making it all but impossible to completely understand their position among the ancient Celts. On the one hand, they were teachers, ritual leaders and scholars, keeping secret lore. This side is widely recognized in modern writings on the organization. However, the other side of the coin is that the Druids were the diplomats, arbiters and judges of their society, helping to keep the often precarious balance of power and peace between rival chiefdoms and factions in what must have been a complex political environment across ancient Gaul, Britain and Ireland.

The Celtic goddess Brid, whose name meant "the exalted one," was one of the names of the daughter of the Dagda, the head god of the Irish Celts and the father and chief of the people of Dana (the Tuatha Dé Danann). Legend claims that she was born at the exact moment of daybreak and rose into the sky with the rays of the sun beaming from her head. As an infant, she was fed with the milk of a sacred cow from the Otherworld.

Brid was also associated with poetry, learning, metal arts, water, and fire. She was most closely concerned with the arts and poetry, but Brid was also known as a goddess of the ordinary people, concerned with healing and agriculture. For this reason, folklore surrounding her survived as it was passed down orally from generation to generation.

Henri Moreau's pictures of a 2ⁿᵈ century BCE statue depicting Brid

Ancient Ireland was often a violent, war-ravaged place where rival clans fought each other for territory and raided each other's villages for plunder and prisoners, who were taken as slaves. Brid transcended territorial disputes, however, by providing some unity among the warring tribes. One of her most ancient names is Breo-Saighead, meaning "fiery arrow," which is associated with punishment and justice. In modern Britain, she is known as the warrior-maiden Brigantia (or Britannia), venerated as an authority on justice. Her likeness is featured on two British coins, and she is central to many heroic myths.

The Life of Brigid

According to Irish historian A.J. Mullowney, the early Irish Christian Church was not as hostile to the Druidic religion as other pagan religions, so it didn't seek to eliminate Druid practices, but to assimilate them into Christian life instead. As a result, while the Celtic gods were reduced to "fairies," their names and attributes were preserved in an oral tradition that survived for hundreds of years after Christianity became firmly established. The Christian approach to the Celtic *filidh*, poets and prophets of the Druid religion, seems to have been to allow them to maintain some literary, historical, and legal responsibilities while suppressing their ritualistic roles. Some of the more popular Celtic deities were absorbed into the Christian tradition as local saints, and the rituals associated with their worship remain as folk customs even in recent times. Early Christian leaders sometimes chose to use what was familiar and comforting to the pagans to attract them to the new religion, rather than push them away by forcing them to give up what they had always known.

According to Mullowney, this is what happened, to some extent, in the case of Brigid of Kildare. Perhaps a baby born in an Irish farming village was simply named for the goddess Brid and what happened later in her life was coincidental, or perhaps attributes of the beloved goddess Brid were later given to a generous and loving nun in an Irish convent. Mullowney noted that the cult of the Druid goddess Brid was established in Celtic Britain long before Christianity arrived, and the revered figure made the transition from pagan goddess to Christian saint with the widespread adoption of the new religion.

Due to the lack of written records at the time, historians cannot know for certain, but either way, the story of Saint Brigid of Kildare is a phenomenal one. She became known throughout Ireland as "Mary of the Gaels," perhaps because Brigid was the Mother Goddess of the Druids. Mothers were given the utmost reverence in ancient Celtic society, which explains how women enjoyed more equality with men than in many other societies at the time. For example, Irish law provided extensively for the rights of women in marriage. Saint Brigid, though she remained a virgin her whole life, was seen as the mother of all Ireland for her caring and nurturing ways, and also because she fostered Christianity in Ireland in its infancy.

According to folklore, Brigid served as midwife at the birth of Jesus and placed three drops of water on his forehead, and that she took him as a foster child to protect him from the slaughter of male infants instigated by Herod. These myths, of course, cannot be possible since she was born more than 400 years after Christ, but they serve to reflect the level of her reverence in early Irish Christian society.

Legend has it that Brigid was the only biological child of Dubtach, king of the Fothairt people of southern Gael whose name means "The Dark One," a demanding and powerful man descended from "Con of the Hundred Battles." The Fothairts were an agricultural people who grew crops and raised cattle and sheep, and their homes and buildings were made of wood or stone, with heather-thatched roofs. Brigid's mother, Broicsesh, was a slave of Dubtach who believed in the new Christian faith, although most Irish people still followed the ancient Druidic religion, including Dubtach himself. According to Whitley Stokes' book, *Lives of Saints*, when Broicsesh was pregnant with Brigid, a local wizard told her that the child in her womb would be marvelous and radiant, and that she would "shine like a sun among the stars of heaven."

Brigid was born in what is known today as Faughart, a land of rich, level farmlands in Upper County Louth around the year 453. One legend claims that she was born in the doorway of a house belonging to a Druid, placing her on a literal threshold between the pagan and Christian worlds.

Both the Hill of Faughart, a historical landmark, and nearby Saint Brigid's Shrine remain popular sites for modern pilgrimages today. Some stories claim that Broicsesh was sold after Brigid was born while Brigid remained with Dubtach's household, and some claim that Brigid remained with her mother throughout her childhood.

Even as a young child, Brigid was distinguished for her virtues of generosity, modesty, kindness, and charity. According to Mullowney, miracles illustrating this were associated with her from early childhood. As a girl, she worked in the village dairy. She often gave milk and butter to the local poor, so much so that sometimes none remained for her own family. Fearing she would be punished for giving away the family's goods, she began to pray. When Broicsesh arrived at the dairy, she found an abundance of milk and butter, and praised the dairy maids for their industry. In another legend, Brigid filled containers of butter only half-full, but when she gave them to her mistress, they were suddenly filled to the top.

In another legend, she turned water from the well into ale, which healed her sick nursemaid.

Brigid was also known for her love of animals; many stories were told of her kindness to stray and starving animals such as the time she gave her father's meager supply of bacon to a stray hound, only to find that it had been miraculously replenished when he asked for it.

Another miracle describes how she was protected by the Holy Spirit even as a child. Supposedly, her mother went out one morning, leaving young Brigid asleep in the house. The neighbors saw a towering fire and billowing smoke rising from her house, but when they arrived to rescue her, there was no fire to be seen, and all was well.

According to Hugh de Blacam's book, *The Saints of Ireland*, Brigid was chosen by God as a young girl. During the time she was living with her father, who followed the Druid religion, she attended some sort of Christian gathering with a neighbor, which was her first exposure to the new religion. While there, the priest swore that he had seen a vision of the Virgin Mary in which she looked exactly like Brigid.

As an adolescent, Brigid was taught to wield a sword, as were most girls and boys in her time, since the militaristic Gaelic people often engaged in territorial disputes. After all, Dubtach was known for the ferocity and frequency of his raiding parties for slaves in Britannia. But despite their violent ways, some Fothairt were Christians, and Brigid may have been raised in a Christian household and educated with the Scriptures. Her mother or father even reportedly took her to see Saint Patrick preach, and some say she was baptized by Saint Patrick himself.

In *Life of Saint Brigid, Virgin,* John O'Hanlon asserted that Brigid did hear Saint Patrick preach as a girl, and she fell into a stupor and had a vision of the future church of Ireland. He also claimed that she was very devout, even as a child, and made her own altar out of a stone, which an angel helped her construct. It was said that Brigid received an excellent education as a child, and that she was always mature and serious, never engaging in frivolous or sophomoric pursuits, but always focused on improving her relationship with God through prayer, study, and service.

As a young girl, Brigid visited the King of Leinster, the province where she lived with her family. The king had several harps hung about his great hall although no one at court knew how to play them. Brigid blessed the hands of some of the people who lived at court and they immediately began playing beautiful music. The king was enchanted and offered to give Brigid anything she wanted in return. Without hesitation, she asked for all the prisoners to be released instead of requesting some material object for herself, which the king probably would have been happier to give.

When Brigid reached marriageable age, which was about 12 at the time, she decided to enter the religious life instead of marrying the son of a noble chosen by her father, much to his dismay. She was harshly treated by members of her family and village since her marriage would have been to their political and economic advantage. According to one legend, she gouged out her own eye to make herself unmarriageable, and when he saw her level of devotion, her father assured her she would not be forced to marry. She immediately washed the blood from her face, and when she removed her hands, her eye had reappeared just as it was before. Another legend says that she prayed that God would make her so ugly that no suitor would have her, and she awoke one morning to find her face badly disfigured. Her good looks returned once her father agreed to let her take the veil, which is another term for taking the vows of a nun, as holy women at the time were required to always keep their heads covered.

Mullowney wrote that Brigid and up to seven other girls left their homes and traveled to County Meath to the church of Bishop Maccaille to devote themselves to Christ as nuns. She could have been as young as fourteen at this time, since this was the earliest age girls were allowed to receive the veil by decree, but O'Hanlon claims that she was 16. There was a large congregation in the church when the girls entered to pray, and they all reported seeing a column of fire resting on Brigid's head and rising to the roof of the church. The bishop, who had been hesitant to consecrate the girls, since they were young and he did not know them, immediately accepted them all. According to O'Hanlon, when Brigid touched the wood on the altar as she kneeled to receive her veil, it sprang forth with green growth again, and, years later, when that same church burned down, only the portion she touched escaped the flames.

Up to this time, there were no religious houses for women in Ireland. Those who decided to devote themselves to God by remaining virgins lived at home with their parents or with friends and performed ordinary household duties. Brigid changed all this.

The church where Brigid was consecrated, on Croghan Hill in present-day County Westmeath, became the site of the first convent in Ireland. She and her fellow postulants, or candidates seeking admission into a religious order, were given a small house to live in and cows to raise. Soon, according to O'Hanlon, many other women, both virgins and widows, were so inspired by Brigid's story that they also sought to embrace the life of a nun by joining her.

Once Brigid and her companions completed their novitiate, the probationary period before becoming a nun, they journeyed about 30 miles to Ardagh, where they made their final vows to Saint Mel, the nephew of Saint Patrick. Here they founded another convent and stayed for twelve years, during which time the convent thrived. Many ladies took the veil, following in Brigid's footsteps, and she sent them to various parts of Ireland to establish new foundations.

Brigid then set off on a journey around Ireland, visiting Saint Patrick and other churches and religious orders, founding new convents and performing miracles wherever she went. The elders from her home province of Leinster repeatedly asked her to return and make her home amongst them, offering her any site in the province. She chose Drum Criadh ("the ridge of clay") near the River Liffey, in what is now the town of Kildare, about 30 miles west of Dublin, around the year 480. On the ridge stood a majestic oak tree, and Brigid decided to build her chapel beneath its branches.

This is one instance of ancient Druid practices interspersing with a Christian premise as the Druids were especially fond of oak trees and supposedly chose them for spiritual rituals. Is it a coincidence, then, that Brigid's most sacred location was also founded near an oak tree? Perhaps early Christians used the oak as a common thread to attract unsure pagans to the new religion. The new foundation became known as Cill Dara (eventually becoming Kildare), which means "Church of the Oak." Or perhaps, Brigid chose an oak grove in which to establish her monastery because the trees were already associated with religious practice. Whether she chose the site independently or not, many early Christian establishments were built on the sites of older pagan worship. According to Elizabeth Rees's book, *Celtic Saints of Ireland*, the tree survived until the 10th century.

Legend has it that Brigid asked the king of the province for as much land around the oak as her cloak would cover. This obviously being a small amount, the king quickly agreed. Brigid removed her woolen cloak and spread it on the ground. To the astonishment of everyone watching, the cloak miraculously expanded and grew, stretching in all four directions at once. When it stopped, it covered about twelve square miles of rich, green pastureland, which is known today as the Curragh, a picturesque area known for horse rearing and racing. The king was amazed, realizing that Brigid was truly blessed by God. He supplied money and resources to build the monastery and even converted to Christianity.

The first building of the new establishment was probably made of wattle - wooden branches interlaced with sticks and twigs to hold them together - and was a rudimentary home and chapel for Brigid and her Sisters. But soon, as its reputation and the fame of its holy founder spread, many pious women came seeking admission to the house, and there was need to enlarge the original building. In addition to novitiates, religious men and women came to visit and confer with Brigid on matters of religious concern. Soon, construction began on a larger monastery, with labor and materials furnished completely through charity from the King of Leinster, neighboring people, pilgrims, and visitors.

The nunnery and chapel that Brigid founded subsequently became the Cathedral of Saint Brigid of Kildare, and Brigid became the first Abbess of Kildare. Over time, the village of Kildare grew around the monastery, as those helped or healed by Brigid chose to build homes near her, and the work of the order expanded to require outside laborers. Many also chose to move to Kildare because Brigid had established the entire town as a place of safety for outcasts and refugees. Eventually, six different roads were established, all converging on Kildare Cathedral, and the city became an important one.

The new foundation prospered and developed rapidly, according to Mullowney, becoming known as a great center of learning and the arts with influence over a wide territory. Girls came from all parts of Ireland and even abroad to join the Brigidine community. Bishops and priests journeyed to Cill Dara to seek Brigid's advice and guidance. A most unusual double monastery developed, where monks and nuns lived on the same site, with Brigid as head of the sisterhood, and Bishop Conleth leading the brothers, although it seems that Brigid held most of the sway over both communities. For this reason, she is venerated today as a symbol of gender equality and feminine leadership.

The monastery also became a home to poets, artists, farmers, and craftsmen, as well as a way station for travelers and vagabonds. Brigid's warm hospitality was known all over the countryside, and she welcomed everyone, whether Christian or not, and fed them and housed them for as long as they needed. In the most basic Christian tradition, every guest is seen as a representative of Christ and should be treated with the utmost respect and care, and Brigid always lived by this tenet.

Brigid continued to perform miracles after her consecration as well, according to Stokes. She healed consumptives, lunatics, and lepers, calmed storms, turned water into milk and stone into salt, returned sight to the blind and speech to the dumb. At times, she was able to see Satan and speak with him, driving him away from her people. She supposedly taught a fox to dance and tamed a wild boar. When a local noblewoman refused to give apples from her orchard to the poor, Brigid cursed her orchard, and it never produced fruit again. One of her fellow nuns, Dara, went blind, but her sight was restored when Brigid prayed for it. Upon regaining her vision, Dara claimed that the clarity of sight blurred God in the eye of her soul, and she asked Brigid to return her to blindness, so that she could see God more clearly.

  For centuries, according to David Atherton and Michael Peyton's article, "Saint Brigid: Holy Wells, Patterns, and Relics," Kildare was run by a double line of male abbot-bishops and female abbesses, with the abbess serving as the head of the establishment. One story tells that Brigid was inadvertently ordained as a bishop when Bishop Mel accidentally used the Latin word for "bishop" at her ordination ceremony instead of the word for "nun." When some of the men objected that the bishop's orders should not be conferred on a woman, Mel told them that the dignity had been conferred on Brigid by God, and he could not disobey. Whether this was an accident or not, Brigid was recognized in her lifetime as a bishop of the church, an unusual honor, as only men can be ordained as Catholic priests or bishops, even to this day. This is proved by the canonical records at Armagh that recognize Brigid's authority throughout her province. Brigid was the only female at her time who performed the mass, consecrated the eucharist, heard confessions, and ordained clergy.

For the next seven centuries, abbesses of Kildare held episcopal status as bishops. This power structure, the only one of its kind in Europe, was one of the many features of the early Irish Church that distinguished it from other Catholic establishments in Europe. Unfortunately, the Synod of Kells-Mellifont, an assembly of the national clergy, ended the practice in 1152, but the Abbess of Kildare continued to be regarded as the Superioress General, or highest authority nun, in all the convents of Ireland.

At this time, monasteries were responsible for their own sustainability, so they raised crops and livestock not only for their use, but also to aid the poor in the community. The convent raised sheep on the rich green hills of the Curragh, and Brigid was known to tend the flocks herself as they grazed on the grounds around the convent. According to de Blacam, the sisters at Kildare spun and wove their own cloth from the wool of their sheep to make their habits, which were most likely natural-colored homespun wool as the wool was easy to dye and virtually waterproof.

The priests and nuns who resided at Saint Brigid's monastery lived in beehive-shaped huts called clochans, which were made from wattle or shaped rocks that fit together without mortar. Each religious person had their own clochan for sleeping, meditating, and praying. There were separate buildings for communal dining and working, depending on the task. The buildings were grouped together for protection close to a ringed stone fort in which the animals were kept and which also acted as a place to defend the community when under attack, though Brigid maintained peaceful relationships with the local chieftains as a method of protection and peace. A high stone wall with several gated openings encircled the monastery grounds. As more and more devoted people came to live at the expanding monastery, the town of Kildare grew around it. It was quite a metropolitan city for pre-medieval Europe.

Miracles of Saint Brigid abound, and while they might seem implausible to modern readers, they provide a description of Saint Brigid that is wholly credible, as well as a greater understanding of her era. They might be stories based on fact and embellished by the vivid Celtic imagination, but these miracles reflect the national feeling and popular opinion which widely prevailed during the times they were written, underscoring how Brigid's followers viewed her, as an enlightened woman chosen by God who helped to bring about monumental change to their way of life.

Many of the stories told of Brigid revolve around the tasks of ordinary life, including milking cows, making butter, harvesting crops, and brewing ale. For instance, a local legend claimed that she once provided enough ale for 18 churches for four days from a single barrel. During one harvest, a torrential storm forced workers on all neighboring farms to stop their labors, but not a drop fell on her land, and the harvest was brought in on schedule. These and other similar tales emphasize the dignity of home life and what was traditionally seen as women's work, shattering the divide between what is ordinary and what is divine. For this reason, Brigid was venerated by common people toiling in the Irish countryside to provide for their families, while her status as an educated daughter of a nobleman helped her appeal to the upper classes as well, and her piousness and miraculous abilities exalted her with the clergy class - she truly was a saint for all of God's people.

   Brigid also spent a great deal of time traveling around the countryside in a chariot, working as a healer to the sick and injured. She once restored feeling to a man's hand that had been paralyzed. A young girl who had been mute all her life suddenly gained the ability to speak when Brigid asked her a question. She healed lepers by sprinkling water on them and helped a paralytic boy to walk again. A paralyzed woman became healed just by sitting in Brigid's shadow. Some of these "patients" welcomed her as an incarnation of the pagan goddess Brigid, and she used her time to gently minister to them and convert them to Christianity, insisting that these miracles came from God alone, as she was merely a vessel of His love and glory. O'Hanlon writes that her efforts resulted in the conversion of a great many pagans and helped solidify the beliefs of those newly converted to the faith.

Like Saint Patrick, Brigid spent much of her time traveling around Ireland, establishing communities of nuns as well as preaching to the people and converting them to Christianity. In her travels, several followers accompanied her, one of whom always remained behind to preside over a newly established community. She worked hard to assure that girls and women were allowed to receive an education, something unheard of at that time. Taking the veil soon became an emblem of Gaelic womanhood that would last for centuries.

Once, while traveling, she and her companions came to the River Shannon, Ireland's largest river. The ferryman requested an exorbitant fee to take them across the river, so Brigid and her party proceeded to walk across, the normally deep water miraculously never reaching higher than their knees. She once fell out of her chariot and smashed her head upon a rock, but did not die.

Cill Dara, like the other communities Brigid established, was primitive in its manner of living and also in the severity of its rules and discipline, as the women who lived there were expected to sacrifice everything for the glory of God, including all comforts, possessions, and selfish pursuits. Nuns lived in very simple cells, and spent their time in prayer, labor, study, and acts of charity, clothing the naked and feeding the hungry. These convents became a house of refuge for the many poor in Ireland, and they never left empty-handed. This spirit of generosity and love displayed by the Christians undoubtedly had a positive influence on the pagans, especially since the solace they offered contrasted so greatly to their former lives of violence, inequality, and hardship under Celtic tribal conflicts. It is said that Saint Brendan, Saint Kevin, and Saint Finian all lived at Kildare as young men and were trained under Saint Brigid's leadership.

At some point, Brigid was said to have found her mother, who was still a slave, and purchased her freedom. She subsequently took her mother to live with her at Kildare.

No exact date for Saint Brigid's death is recorded, but it is believed that she died on February 1st around the age of 70, making the year of her death about 523. According to O'Hanlon, she was attended while dying by Saint Ninnidh, known as Ninnidh of the Clean Hand, who had his right hand encased with a metal covering to prevent it from ever being defiled after the first time he ever touched Saint Brigid. Years earlier, Brigid foretold that Ninnidh would be present at her death and would give her the last rites, and he spent years away from her in order to preserve her life, as well as encasing his hand so that the last hands to touch her would be pristine.

A painting depicting Saint Brigid's death

After her death, Brigid's cult quickly grew. Around 650, the Kildare monk Cogitosus wrote the *Life of Brigid,* from which historians and Catholic scholars obtain most information about her. According to Rees, this it is the earliest surviving biography of any Irish saint. He writes that vast crowds came to Kildare from all over Ireland each year on February 1st to bring offerings to Saint Brigid, to pray to her for healing, and to celebrate her life. Her community came to hold jurisdiction over a large part of southwest Ireland until the suppression of the monasteries in the 16th century.

Another early writing about Brigid is Ultán's Hymn, one of the oldest hymns in the Irish language, dating from the 7th century and combining pagan and Christian motifs. Part of it reads:

> "Brigit, woman ever excellent, golden, radiant flame,
>
> Lead us to the eternal kingdom, the brilliant, dazzling sun.
>
> May Brigit guide us past crowds of devils,
>
> May she break before us the attack of every plague.
>
> May she destroy within us the taxes of our flesh,
>
> The branch with blossoms, the mother of Jesus.
>
> The true virgin, easy to love, with great honour,
>
> I shall be forever safe with my saint of Leinster."

Conversion

***Elke Wetzig's* picture of a statue of Brigid**

In the days of early Christianity, priests and monks were sent out from Rome to spread the new religion to all parts of the Roman Empire, which included Gael, as Ireland was known at the time. In the 5th century, Rome had a loose hold upon many of its outposts, especially Gael, as it was far away over the sea and entrenched under the rule of many tribal leaders. However, Christianity took hold quite easily on the Emerald Isle, perhaps not only because

Druidic customs honored hospitality to guests, but also because Patrick delivered his message in the terms of the Gaelic people. He spoke Gaelic and taught of the gospel in a language they could understand. Also, he did not alienate those he sought to convert by asking them to give up their ancient customs but converted some of those customs to Christian use. He often sought out respected upper-class women to convert, knowing their great influence over the rest of society.

   Therefore, the conversion of Ireland was accomplished without any bloodshed, which is unique to the early church, which often encountered insurmountable obstacles and trials wherever it went. Early missionaries were often attacked and killed, or Roman armies invaded and converted the natives by force when the clergy faced a great deal of opposition.

   After the fall of Rome in 476, barbarians ravaged Europe and its people, pillaging valuables and burning all books and art. Up to this point, Irish monastic scribes preserved and made copies of every Christian and Classical book they could, a painstaking task that took lots of time and manpower to accomplish. Without the religious orders founded by Brigid, Patrick, and other Irish saints, many important texts would not exist today.

Knowles also writes that Brigid "infused a vigor and energy into the Irish Church which it maintains down to the present day. Her works of charity relieved distress in many an Irish home." She continued Saint Patrick's work of converting the pagan Irish after his death, strengthening the churches he had begun and helping new ones to sprout and flourish.

By the late 6th century, enthusiasm for the new Christian religion led many Irish men and women to devote themselves to the austere monastic life and to serve as missionaries to pagan tribes in Scotland, northern England, and west-central Europe. By the 7th century, a comprehensive monastic system developed in Ireland.

After the Reformation of the early 16th century, Catholicism became closely associated with Irish nationalism and resistance to British rule as King Henry VIII separated his kingdom from the Catholic Church. Ireland's patron Catholic saints, Brigid, Patrick, and Columba, became emblems of Irish culture and independence as well as icons of religion.

Every Catholic saint has their own icon or pictorial representation, and Sister Aloysius McVeigh was commissioned by the Parish of Kildare to paint a new icon for Saint Brigid in 2001. Unlike a portrait, an icon seeks to represent the saint's spiritual essence through symbols.

In her left hand, Brigid holds a picture of her monastic foundation in front of the famous oak that gives Cill Dara its name. Her love of learning is depicted by an open book. Under Brigid's foot is pictured a jeweled sword, perhaps the one she gave away to feed a poor family, signifying her renunciation of wealth and abhorrence of violence. Also depicted are a flame representing Saint Brigid's fire and a brooch representing her school of metalwork and art.

Saint Brigid's Cross is shown in green as they are traditionally made from fresh grasses with symbols of each Gospel writer, a lion representing Mark, an eagle for John, an ox for Luke, and an angel representing Matthew. Saint Brigid is shown with a red halo, similar to contemporary depictions of the Virgin Mary because Brigid was known as Mary of the Gael. Brigid holds a bishop's crozier in her right hand, symbolizing her dignity as an abbess.

To Brigid's right, small cows and milk buckets are shown, symbolizing Brigid's association with livestock and dairies. Brigid worked alongside her mother in the village dairy throughout childhood, and her monastery also featured a thriving dairy which supplied milk, butter, and cheese to the locals. According to legend, the cattle of the monastery were able to be milked three times a day, rather than twice as is the normal practice, in order to supply enough milk to everyone in need.

On the site of the original convent, visitors will find the legendary Saint Brigid's Fire which burns in a large metal bowl that reportedly never goes out. According to Giraldus Cambrensis's writings from 1186, the 20 sisters of the convent took nightly turns tending it and feeding it with watchful and diligent care. After Brigid's death, the fire continued burning during her turn although no one took her place. Each sister took care of the fire for a single night, leaving the 20th night for Brigid. The 19th sister adds wood on the 20th night, and on the 20th morning, the nuns awake to find the fire still burning and the usual amount of fuel used, but no accumulation of ashes. Supposedly, no ashes ever accumulate as the fire burns.

Like other symbols associated with Brigid, the fire originated in pre-Christian times as a sacred fire tended by nineteen Druid priestesses called "daughters of the flame," according to Atherton and Peyton. These priestesses invoked the goddess Brigid to protect their herds and to provide a fruitful harvest. Scholars suggest that priestesses in ancient times gathered on the hill of Kildare to tend ritual fires while invoking the goddess Brigid to protect their herds and provide a fruitful harvest.

When Saint Brigid built her monastery and church in Kildare, she continued the custom of keeping the fire alight but invoked it as a symbol of the Holy Spirit, as fire has been associated with the Holy Spirit since the Pentecost when the Holy Spirit descended on the apostles soon after Christ's resurrection. The fire's perpetual light became a symbol of the Holy Spirit's constant presence in people's lives as well as a symbol of Christ, the one true light in the dark world.

The fire was supposedly surrounded by a hedge which no male was ever allowed to enter. According to Mullowney, men who have attempted to enter the hedge have gone mad, or even lost a limb that got too close.

This fire has been continually burning since 480, except for a few periods in history. In the 13th century, Henry of London, Archbishop of Dublin, ordered the fire to be extinguished because he considered it a pagan ritual. It was also extinguished during the Reformation under Henry VIII, but it was relit at some point each time. In 1993, the flame was relit in the Kildare Market Square by Mary Teresa Cullen, leader of the Brigidine Sisters. Since then, the fire has been tended by the sisters in their center, Solas Bhride. Each year, the flame burns in the town square for the duration of the Festival of Saint Brigid.

In 2006, the Kildare County Council commissioned a sculpture to house the fire, a twisted column topped with large metal oak leaves into which is nestled a bronze acorn cup holding the flame. A torch transferred the flame from Solas Bhride to the sculpture in Kildare town Square, where it perpetually burns as a symbol of hope, justice, and peace.

In another amalgamation of pagan and Christian practices, Saint Brigid's feast day, known locally as Féile Bríde, falls on February 1st, the same day as the pagan feast of *Imbolc*, the festival of spring marking the return of fertility to the land. Midway between the winter solstice, and the spring equinox, the day commemorates the reawakening of the earth from its winter slumber, celebrating new beginnings and new life on Earth.

In early agrarian societies in northern climates such as Ireland, winters were an especially difficult season to survive, so the coming of spring was important not only as a sign of better days ahead, but also a celebration of the survival of another dreary battle against the elements.

On the eve of Imbolc in pre-Christian times, all the girls and young women of a village would gather in one house and stay up all night making images of the sun (which came to be known as Saint Brigid's Crosses) and Brídeóg, a doll-like figure of the goddess Brigid made from bundles of oats and rushes, placed in a white dress with a crystal on her chest, and put in a basket. Lamps and bonfires were lit as a tribute to Brigid.

In the morning, the young men would seek permission to enter the house and pay reverence to Brídeóg and request blessings from Brigid. The head of the household would extinguish the nightly fire and the ashes would be inspected for signs that Brigid had entered the house and walked on them. The Brídeóg would be carried from house-to-house in a parade. This ritual was practiced in parts of Ireland up to the mid-20th century.

As Imbolc was replaced with Saint Brigid's Day, new Catholic rituals replaced the pagan ones. An effigy of Saint Brigid is traditionally washed in the ocean and surrounded by candles to dry, and Saint Brigid crosses are made from stalks of wheat.

In another custom, one girl of the village was chosen to be "Brigid," and she carried Brigid's crosses from house to house in a parade-like manner, accompanied by other young girls through the streets. At every door, she was welcomed with a Gaelic greeting to Saint Brigid, and, after an exchange of prayers, she bestowed one of the crosses on each house, where it was hung in the rafters until Saint Brigid's Feast Day the following year.

According to de Blacam, this continued through the 17th century.

Brigid is associated with nature and the earth, as she was attuned to the season and cycles of nature. Stories abound of her performing everyday agricultural tasks: milking the cows, churning the milk, making butter, and brewing ale. Even today, rituals and traditions performed on Saint Brigid's eve and feast day center on the hearth and the home, as people rely on Brigid to keep their homes, animals, and crops safe. Believers look for signs that Saint Brigid has visited their home on the eve of her feast day and blessed it as the occupants sleep.

Believers often hang a woven Saint Brigid's cross over their door or window on Saint Brigid's Eve. The head of the household stands at the door, knocks, and asks to be let in in the name of Brigid. Some communities still make and carry brídeógs into the home. In some places, children go from house to house carrying the brídeóg and are given treats from neighbors. Music, dancing, and a family meal, often featuring corn cakes made from the first and last corn of the harvest are often part of the festivities. Some of the food is placed outside for Saint Brigid's spirit as she passes in the night, and food is often donated to the poor in the morning.

The popular festival is still celebrated today, as a week-long series of events including a candle-lit pilgrimage walk to Saint Brigid's Well, weaving Saint Brigid's crosses, retelling of her legends, art, poetry, music, and Irish dancing. Hundreds of people from all walks of life come to the Shrine of Brigid at Faughart to celebrate and pray. Afri, or Action from Ireland, a national organization that promotes human rights, peace, justice and environmentalism, holds an annual peace and justice conference each year during Feile Brid, showing a modern interpretation of the ideas that Saint Brigid stood for in her lifetime.

One legend purports that Saint Brigid hung her wet laundry on a sunbeam to dry which has ties to the ancient pagan tradition of sun worship. The slanted sun rays transformed into the diagonal lines of Saint Brigid's Cross, traditionally woven from rushes. According to Rees, Brigid's cross likely pre-dates Christianity in an earlier three-armed form, another example of how Brigid's pagan customs were adopted into the new religion.

Legend claims that Saint Brigid was called to the home of a dying pagan leader to share the message of the gospel with him in hopes that he would become a believer before his death. He refused to convert, but she remained with him, talking and praying. As she spoke to him, she took some rushes from the floor and weaved them into the shape of a cross. The man asked what she was doing, and she used the cross as a visual aid to explain the Gospel to him. Full of understanding, he came to the faith and allowed Brigid to baptize him just before he died, ensuring his entrance into heaven.

For centuries, the Irish have continued to make Saint Brigid's crosses which must be constructed from freshly pulled green rushes and woven from left to right. The four arms of the cross are interlocked at the center and the ends are tied in small knots or bound with thread. On Saint Brigid's Day, people bring their crosses to Mass to be blessed and sprinkled with holy water. The crosses can last for years, but when they begin to deteriorate, it is customary to burn them or bury them in a field which is believed to bring a good harvest.

Saint Brigid's Cross

In 1983, five young Irish boys made and sold Saint Brigid's crosses and gave the proceeds to Afri, leading to the launch of the Brigid Peace Cross Campaign by Nobel Peace Prize winner Sean MacBride. Thousands of young people all over Ireland took up the campaign by making crosses which came to symbolize justice, peace, and human rights during a time of great turmoil in Ireland.

Today, many Irish people still place Saint Brigid's crosses in their homes to protect inhabitants from illness and misfortune. The cross is also often hung in barns to bless the cows since Brigid was also a patroness of cattle and milk.

Early churches were always built near natural wells as water was obviously needed for daily life as well as the rite of Baptism which required water that was blessed by a holy man or woman. Therefore, all the Irish saints have at least one well associated with their name.

Numerous wells throughout Ireland and Britain are associated with Saint Brigid, at least fifteen in Ireland alone. One of these, in the plain of Longford, was created, according to legend, during a drought, when Brigid, like a diviner, found water underground, directed her companions to dig at a certain spot, and so opened up a gushing source of fresh water, saving the nearby people and their livestock.

Natural wells were also sites of veneration in the Druidic religion and were purported to have healing properties. According to Atherton and Peyton, the Celts believed that these wells were doorways to the Underworld and the womb of the Mother, the source of all life. Pope Gregory counseled early Irish and British missionaries not to destroy pagan shrines at natural wells but to adopt them for Christian use, another example of pagan rituals being transformed into Christian practices.

The original Brigid's Well is found near the Cliffs of Moher in the town of Tully, about a mile south of Kildare. Since there is no stream in Kildare, the well was used to provide running water for the convent's flour mill. Today, it is marked by a standing stone cross atop a circular stone enclosure around the small pool of water. A nearby tree is hung with "clouties," rags or strips of cloth which pilgrims hang from trees or bushes near a holy well as a request for healing or in gratitude for a cure. Today, the cloutie tree in Tully is adorned with bandages, handkerchiefs, socks, stockings, and children's toys, serving as evidence of silent prayers for healing from various injuries, ailments, and childhood illnesses.

Brigid was also associated with healing, and her wells are still visited by those seeking cures for physical ailments. Several miracles attributed to the saint involve healing as well: a blind man regaining his sight, a dumb girl gaining her speech, many cured lepers and paralytics, and others. Brigid's girdle was supposedly capable of curing all disease and illness, according to Mullowney. Although a lifelong virgin, she was invoked as patron of childbirth by women and revered as a midwife.

The well at Brigid's birthplace, Faughart, is still a popular place of pilgrimage. Pilgrims recite the rosary as they enter the cemetery where the well is located. They then walk three times clockwise around an ash tree reciting The Lord's Prayer and Hail Marys. They then make their way to the well where they kneel in prayer before walking three times around the well and taking a sip of the water therein. Along the path, there are three stones. At the Head Stone, pilgrims lower their head onto the stone and pray for a cure for any ailment of the head. At the Eye Stone, they bathe their eyes in the water. At the Knee Stone, they kneel in the marks on the stone and pray to Saint Brigid for a cure for any physical ailment. Pilgrims often tie small pieces of cloth on the bushes near the well. According to tradition, as the cloth disintegrates in the wind and rain, the petitioner's illnesses are cured.

The last Sunday in July is also celebrated as a patron day when pilgrims assemble at Saint Brigid's Well and spend the whole night there, praying to the saint, worshipping through music, and leaving offerings on the wall outside the well.

Saint Brigid's cloak, which had miraculously spread over hundreds of acres to establish the land for her monastery, is said to cover the entire Curragh of Kildare, providing its inhabitants, both human and animal, with protection and blessings. *Brat Bride Ort*, meaning "the cloak of Brigid upon you," is a popular blessing used throughout Ireland, invoking the protection of Brigid's cloak even today.

On the eve of Saint Brigid's Day, it was customary to leave a piece of cloth outside the house as a symbol of her cloak. It was believed that the saint's spirit traveled across the land through the night and would leave her curative powers in the cloth. The same cloth could then be used throughout the year to heal from sickness and protect from harm.

Fragments of Saint Brigid's cloak, described as dark red or brown pieces of shaggy wool with silver thread running through them, are said to be preserved at the Convent of the Redemptoristines in Drumcondra, near Dublin, and at the Cathedral of Bruges in Belgium. The Bruges cloak, or mantle, as it is called, is said to have come from the English Princess Gunhild who took refuge from invaders in Flanders (present day Belgium) in 1051. At the same time, her brothers went to Ireland and stayed in Leinster, the home of the Shrine of Saint Brigid. It is entirely possible that they obtained a relic of the saint at this time and gave it to their sister. It is first documented in a list of church property in 1347, and it remains in the Cathedral to this day and is displayed each year on Saint Brigid's Day.

The Church that Brigid Built

The Kildare Cathedral has been a site of Christian worship for over 1,500 years, making it one of the oldest such sites in all of Ireland. In his book *Cathedral of Saint*

Brigid of Kildare, Joseph Dollard described the current cathedral as "simple in style but of beautiful proportions," with a grand square tower and unique buttress arches surrounded by picturesque grounds.

A modern picture of the Kildare Cathedral

From 480 until the early 9th century, very little is recorded of the cathedral. Cogitosus, who lived at the Kildare monastery in the 7th century, described the wooden cathedral as large and very lofty and elaborately adorned with paintings. It had three large oratories, or chapels, divided from each other by wooden partitions, called rood screens, and beautifully decorated curtains, with a simple yet splendid altar. The great body of the church was divided into two equal parts, divided by screens, the right one for the male congregation and the left one for the females. This was the normal mode of worship at the time. In this main sanctuary, priests, monks, nuns, pilgrims, townspeople, nobles and peasants all worshipped together.

Cogitosus also describes a high round stone tower with a conical cap and a sculpted high cross. According to O'Hanlon, the 96-foot tall round tower probably represents the exact site of Saint Brigid's early establishment. It is considered to be one of the finest specimens of its era, as well as one of the most celebrated historic sites in Ireland.

Saint Brigid also founded a school of art on the grounds of the monastery, with workshops for manuscript illumination and metalwork. The school became renowned for the high quality of its designs and products. Great masters assembled at Cill Dara to teach science and art, but students also learned virtue and piety through the Scriptures. Other well-known Irish saints often visited, including Saint Patrick. It is said that he and Brigid enjoyed a close relationship; she even wove his burial shroud, according to legend.

The church's claims to fame were the shrines of Saint Brigid and Saint Conlaeth, which were situated at each side of the altar and contained their bodies. The shrines were adorned with wrought gold, gems and precious stones and had gold and silver crowns hanging over them. Pilgrims, who visited in a steady flow throughout the year, donated generous gifts to Brigid's Shrine. In 836, a fleet of thirty Danish, or Viking, ships sailed up the River Liffey and plundered every church and abbey they could find, destroying the town of Kildare, and absconding with the shrines of Brigid and Conlaeth. Luckily, Brigid's remains had been removed the previous year to protect them from Viking invaders. They were taken to Downpatrick and interred in the same tomb as Saint Patrick and Columbkille, Ireland's other patron saints. Soon, Down was invaded too, and her remains were moved again, this time to a location only known to a few priests. Over time, all knowledge of her burial place was lost.

In 1185, Saint Malachy, bishop of Down, sought God's guidance on finding Brigid's remains. According to legend, a beam of light settled over a spot on the floor of the church. When the brothers dug into this spot, they found the graves of not only Saint Brigid, but also Saints Patrick and Columbkille. In 1186, the public translation, or reburial, of the remains of all three saints took place with a ceremony sanctioned by Pope Urban III and attended by a papal legate and several other bishops and clergy at Downpatrick Cathedral.

Saint Brigid's Abbey was known for its scriptorium, where monks studied, copied, illustrated, and celebrated God's Word in a large wooden building with simple tables and window-like openings high up in the walls that admitted a large amount of daylight yet shielded the interior from the weather, so that scribes could work without the need for candles in the daytime. Brigid's scriptorium contained hundreds of illuminated manuscripts, but most were destroyed during Viking raids, of which there were at least 16 by the end of the 10th century. Since the Vikings had no written language and were largely illiterate, they saw no value in the manuscripts and burned most of them.

One of the most interesting stories of the cathedral is an illustrated manuscript supposedly created during Brigid's life. A Norman scribe, Giraldus Cambrensis, writing in 1185, described a beautiful book containing the four Gospels according to Saint Jerome, with colorful drawings on almost every page. The art was so delicate, exquisite, and elaborate, that it was said to be the work of an angel. Local lore claimed that an unnamed scribe composed the translation and an angel supplied the artwork at Brigid's behest, and this manuscript has come to be known as the lost *Book of Kildare*. Scholars believe that it existed prior to the *Book of Kells*, a similar illuminated manuscript of the four Gospels that was created in the 9th century and can now be viewed at Trinity College in Dublin, but the *Book of Kildare* was lost sometime after Cambrensis's visit. Some believe it was stolen or destroyed during the time of Oliver Cromwell's reign over England in the 17th century. Conversely, others believe it still exists and hope it will be unearthed someday.

In the 1st millennium, Irish monasteries became notable centers of learning, as Christianity brought Latin to Ireland, and the works of church fathers and classical authors were read and studied. Irish scribes produced manuscripts written in Insular, a type of calligraphy with initial letters illuminated, or decorated with intricate colorful ribbon and animal designs. The Irish, in fact, led the way in creating illuminated texts. Some scholars believe that the Irish proliferation of these manuscripts and their copies helped re-Christianize the European continent in the Dark Ages after the fall of Rome. Perhaps Saint Brigid can be thanked for this because of her devotion to education and reproduction of the written word in the scriptorium she established at Kildare.

Due to numerous Viking attacks, a civil war, and the ravages of 1,500 years, nothing remains of the early monastery except a nine-foot tall partial high cross made of granite, ruins of the fire structure, and an impressive round tower whose doorway has recessed arches carved in low relief. The Normans invaded and settled Ireland in the late 12th century, and a new early Gothic-style cathedral was built on the grounds of the old one in 1230, featuring a square central tower and a number of defensive features. In 1996, foundations of a small rectangular building were uncovered, which are believed to have been the fire structure. This was named the Fire Temple, with the street beside the cathedral called Fire Temple Lane.

When King Henry VIII separated from the Roman Catholic Church in 1532, he outlawed Catholicism, which meant dissolving all Catholic monasteries, abbeys, and cathedrals and taking possession of all their belongings. At this time, the relics of many saints, including Brigid, were scattered and lost. The cathedral remained unoccupied for decades and fell into disrepair. In 1540, the Brigidine Order went into hiding to avoid Catholic persecution, leaving the grounds of the original cathedral and setting up in the countryside outside Kildare. The Order of Saint Brigid maintained a quiet, almost invisible existence here until 1833 when the Catholic Church of Saint Brigid was built about a block away from the cathedral.

According to the Kildare Heritage Society, the cathedral was totally ruined during the Confederate Wars of the mid-1600s. In was partially rebuilt in 1686, so that the chancel could be used as a church. Most of the other grounds were not maintained.

In 1875, a major reconstruction began that took over 20 years to complete. The chancel was rebuilt along the lines of the original church, the central tower was reconstituted, and the remaining walls of the nave and transepts were restored or replaced, incorporating the remaining elements of the original 13th century design. The entire roof and all windows were also replaced. The resulting structure remains entirely intact today.

The Cathedral of Saint Brigid still sits on the land originally developed by Brigid herself, but it is an Anglican Center. The limestone cathedral sits on a rise above the Kildare town square, its massive central tower rising above a large, double-arched nave. In addition to the Kildare church and cathedral, dozens of religious establishments have been dedicated to Saint Brigid over the centuries.

Although most of Brigid's remains were destroyed or lost, luckily, her skull was reportedly saved and transported by three Irish knights to Portugal during the Crusades of the late 1200s. It still rests in a chapel devoted to her in the Church of Saint John the Baptist in Lumiar, near Lisbon. Farmers in the area regard her as their special patroness, and her feast day is celebrated annually. In 1929, a small portion of the skill was returned to Ireland and placed in a bronze and gold-plated reliquary in Saint Brigid's Parish in Killester, near Dublin. The reliquary, worth more than 10,000 Euros, was stolen from the church in 2014, but parish officials had recently removed the relic and affixed it to a cruciform placed in a safe.

The Church of Sao Roque in Lisbon also claims to have part of Saint Brigid's skull. According to Atherton and Peyton, Emperor Rudolf II of the Holy Roman Empire gave the relic to Juan de Borgia who gave it to the Jesuits of Lisbon in 1588. The relic had been secretly transported to Neustadt, Austria by Irish clergy earlier in the 16th century when Henry VIII ordered the dissolution of the monasteries. Supposedly, a portion of this relic was given to the Church of Saint Brigid at Faughart, her birthplace.

After the destruction of the Downpatrick shrines, a finger and tooth (and possibly other relics) of Saint Brigid were transported to the Abbey of Saint Martin of Tours in Cologne. The tooth was given to the Archbishop of Sydney in 1884 for the Order of Brigidine Sisters, but it has since been misplaced. Another relic of Saint Brigid, her burial shroud, was preserved at the Church of Skryne, Ireland, according to Atherton and Peyton.

Brigidine Sisters

Bishop Daniel Delany founded the Order of the Brigidine Sisters on Saint Brigid's Day, 1807. When the austere Penal Laws were repealed in the last decade of the 18th century, Catholics were permitted to give and receive land and open schools. Bishop Delany, who had been secretly educated and consecrated in France, could finally begin his calling of giving all Irish children a religious and secular education by establishing Catholic congregations throughout the country. After two decades of struggling to acquire land leases from Protestant landlords, he obtained a lease in Tullow and built a simple house. He put out a call for women who had taken vows of chastity to re-found the ancient Order of Saint Brigid of Kildare. Six women between the ages of 25 and 48 answered his call and became the very first Sisters of Saint Brigid.

In her history of the Brigidine Sisters, Rita Minehan writes that Delany instructed them thus: "Without love it is all labour in vain. Do everything in a spirit of love and you will not arrive at journey's end with empty hands." The sisters worked from five a.m. to ten p.m. each day to establish a school for children and a working Catholic Congregation, as well as grow and make their own food and supplies. A few new postulants arrived each year, and by 1812, an extension had to be built to house them all.

Delany died in 1814, but the foundations he began continued to flourish. By 1824, the school had enough pupils to justify building a new two-story educational building, and the sisters began making and selling buttons to help pay for it.

In 1837, the Brigidine Sisters established one of the first Catholic boarding schools in Ireland, which enjoyed great success, as the Penal Laws had outlawed Catholic education, and parents were eager to educate their children after their appeal. The order earned a reputation for their system of religious and secular education and attracted a great number of young ladies from all parts of Ireland.

In 1809, Delany established a second Brigidine foundation in Mountrath, and a boarding school was added here also in 1837. A third community was founded in Roscrea in 1823, the first in the Killaloe Diocese since the Reformation. Four other communities were founded across Ireland by the end of the 19th century.

In 1851, two Brigidine sisters left for America. They settled in Kenosha, Wisconsin, and founded a convent that thrived for eighteen years until it was destroyed in a fire. In 1883, Saint Brigid's oak branches spread all the way to Australia when Bishop Murray of Maitland, New South Wales, requested help from the Brigidines to conduct schools, and six sisters set sail for the faraway land. Despite the hardships of heat, disease, lack of resources, and general homesickness, the sisters thrived, and the school was a success. They were even able to send four of their order to establish a new community in Cooma. In 1886, four sisters were sent from Tullow to set up a branch of the Brigidine Order in Echuca, Australia. Three other communities were established in Australia by the end of the 19th century. In 1898, six sisters crossed the Tasman Sea to establish a Brigidine Foundation in New Zealand.

In the 20th century, new orders and missions were established in Wales, England, Papua New Guinea, Mexico, Kenya, Iceland, South America, Bangladesh, the Philippines, China, and Texas. In all of these areas, the Brigidine Sisters continued to minister to parishes, schools, hospitals, and prisons, working with indigenous children and children with special needs, living in housing estates alongside the people they served in disadvantaged areas both in modern nations and the developing world. The Brigidine Order continues its work today, as the oaks planted from tiny acorn seeds continue to grow.

Since that time, the order, which has foundations all over the world, have modeled their lives and work on that of St. Brigid. Bishop Delany originally took acorns from the original Kildare site to plant oak trees at the founding place of the new Brigidine Sisters in Tullow. Today, acorns from Tullow are used to plant oak trees at Brigidine schools and churches all over the world.

St. Brigid's Legacy

Cogitosus's writings, which he composed just a century after her death and are thus considered a mostly contemporary source, place great emphasis on Brigid's faith, healing powers, hospitality, generosity, and compassion for the poor and oppressed. Over 70% of his book discusses her extraordinary concern for the poor.

One such legend, as told by the Order of the Brigidine Sisters, illustrates this compassion perfectly. Once, during her travels, she received a basket of apples from a noble woman. She immediately gave the apples to the poor, telling the woman, "What's mine is theirs." Another legend says that she gave her horses away to a family on the road who was traveling on foot and carrying many heavy loads of goods. She washed the feet of the elderly and ailing nuns at another convent once, restoring them to health.

According to one legend, Brigid gave away the Italian vestments Bishop Conleth used during Mass to some beggars needing clothes. Upon realizing Conleth's displeasure, she prayed to God with great fervor, and new vestments miraculously appeared!

Many other authors composed books about Brigid's life, known as hagiographies, including her chaplain, Saint Ninnidh, who wrote about miracles he witnessed during the time he spent with her. Saint Fiacc supposedly wrote a brief hagiography of Brigid while she was still alive. Saint Brendan, Columba, and Kilian wrote about her life in poems, some of which survived only through oral tradition. These and other hagiographies are not historical documents – they are genre all their own meant to bolster Christianity through the stories of the saints - but they serve to give the modern reader and believer a glimpse into life in the 1st millennium, as well as a sense of how Christianity spread through the practices and actions of the saints. They also give us a way to trace the leading events of a saint's life, such as locations they lived in and traveled to and a general timeline of when major events happened.

Brigid was also known as a peacemaker. Feuds between clans were common, and she often intervened in disputes between rival factions to avoid violence and bring about peaceful reconciliation. In some parts of Ireland, a Saint Brigid's cross is used as a token of goodwill between neighbors. As a child, she is said to have given her father's precious jeweled sword to a beggar suffering from leprosy so that he could barter it for food for his family. In this way, Brigid transformed a weapon of war into a life-giving instrument, symbolizing both her peacefulness and her compassion.

According to de Blacam, a poem dating from the 8th century is said to be a translation of Brigid's own writings which were passed down through the years. One line reads, "I would like the people of Heaven in my house; I would like the baskets of peace to be theirs."

Another story tells of a deceitful man who lent a silver brooch to a woman and then secretly took it back, then blamed her for losing it, making her indebted to him and forced to be his slave to work off the value of the brooch. To ensure that the brooch would not be found, the man threw it into the sea. The accused woman ran to the monastery at Kildare for refuge. Brigid soon found the brooch inside a fish recently brought to the convent by a fisherman, took it to the man and proved, through witnesses, that it was the missing brooch, releasing the woman from slavery.

It is also said that she was especially devoted to showing others mercy, as evidenced by her ministry to prisoners. She washed the feet of lepers and traveled all over Ireland to win the release of captives, as Celtic tribes at the time often engaged in raids to take other tribespeople as slaves. One example, as described by Stokes, tells how Brigid went to the province of Fir Ross to ask the king to release a captive. He refused, but he allowed Brigid to see the prisoner and pray for him. When she did, his chains fell away and the captive fled.

Despite all her fame and power, Brigid remained extremely humble. According to O'Hanlon, she would often spend the entire night wading in a freezing pond in penitence for her sins. It is said that the Almighty Himself showed her his forgiveness by draining the water from the pond at sundown and bringing it back in the morning.

According to Reverend J.A. Knowles's book, *Saint Brigid: Patroness of Ireland,* devotion to Brigid grew after her death and spread all across Ireland, making her the figure most beloved by the Irish people, after only Saint Patrick, "She was the light that shone over their island to direct the footsteps of the daughters of Erin in the paths of virtue and sanctity."

Today, Brigid remains the patroness of parishes, towns, counties, churches, abbeys, and monasteries all over the world. Her influence spans the globe, not only in Ireland and Britain, but as far away as Australia and New Zealand, as well as the United States and Canada. Brigid and Saint Patrick are seen as the pillars on which Christian Ireland stands, part of the great tapestry that makes the nation what it is today. But she is truly a patroness of people everywhere. She brought houses of peace to a war-torn land. She represents many dualities, but she blends them together seamlessly. She's depicted as half-royal, half-slave; half-bishop, half-servant; modest and chaste, yet willful; authoritative, yet humble; capable of miracles, yet happy to do menial work. Although an ancient figure, she has succeeded in traveling through millennia and across continents. She is associated with various aspects of life at the same time, from the art of poetry to the drudgery of housekeeping. Her fire represents the Holy Spirit as well as the blacksmith's forge. She represents the gentle love of Christ as well as the fierce spirit of an independent woman.

In essence, regardless of religion, nationality, gender, race, age, or economic status, Brigid's story should inspire everyone to be kinder to people.

Online Resources

Other books about Catholic history by Charles River Editors

Other books about medieval history by Charles River Editors

Other books about St. Brigid on Amazon

Bibliography

Atherton, David and Peyton, Michael. "Saint Brigid: Holy Wells, Patterns, and Relics." 2015.

Cymres, Winter. "Brigid: Survival of a Goddess." https://druidry.org/brigid.

De Blacam, Hugh. "The Saints of Ireland: The Life-Stores of S.S. Brigid and Columcille." The Bruce Publishing Company, Milwaukee. 2012.

Knowles, J.A., Rev. St. Brigid: Patroness of Ireland. Brown and Nolan, Ltd. Dublin. 1907.

Minehan, Rita, csb. "From the Acorn to the Oak: Celebrating the Brigidine Story." 2010.

Mullowney, A.J. "Brigid - Saint or Goddess." Kildare Archeological Society. 1 February 2017.

Rees, Elizabeth. Celtic Saints of Ireland. The History Press. Gloucestershire. 2013.

Roberts, Clayton and Roberts, David. A History of England: Prehistory to 1714. Prentice-Hall, Inc. Englewood Cliffs, New Jersey. 1991.

Rogers, Rosemary. "Wild Irish Women: Saint Brigid - Mary of the Gaels." https://irishamerica.com/2018/01/wild-irish-women-saint-brigid-mary-of-the-gaels/

Stokes, Whitley. Lives of Saints from the Book of Lismore. . Clarendon Press. Oxford. 1890.

Williment, Paul. "Brighid, Goddess and Saint: Imbolc and other traditions."

https://www.brighid.org.uk/customs.html

Free Books by Charles River Editors

We have brand new titles available for free most days of the week. To see which of our titles are currently free, click on this link.

Discounted Books by Charles River Editors

We have titles at a discount price of just 99 cents everyday. To see which of our titles are currently 99 cents, click on this link.

Manufactured by Amazon.ca
Acheson, AB

15791222R00046